# SHOW ME COOL MAGIC

A guide to creating
and performing
your own show

## Jake Banfield

Quarto is the authority on a wide range of topics.
Quarto educates, entertains and enriches the lives of
our readers—enthusiasts and lovers of hands-on living.
www.quartoknows.com

© 2019 Quarto Publishing plc
First published in 2019 by QED Publishing
an imprint of The Quarto Group.
The Old Brewery, 6 Blundell Street,
London N7 9BH, United Kingdom.
T (0)20 7700 6700 F (0)20 7700 8066
www.QuartoKnows.com

A catalogue record for this book is available from the British Library.

ISBN: 978-1-78603-408-3

Manufactured in Guangdong, China CC022019
9 8 7 6 5 4 3 2 1

Photography: Simon Pask
Project Editor: Emily Pither
Editorial Director: Laura Knowles
Editorial Assistant: Lydia Watson
Designer: Joost Baardman
Art Director: Susi Martin
Creative Director: Malena Stojic
Publisher: Maxime Boucknooghe
Production: Nikki Ingram

MIX
Paper from
responsible sources
FSC® C008047

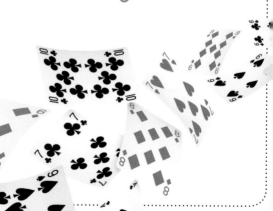

# CONTENTS

# FOREWORD

Who says magic has to be all about top hats and rabbits? Magic can be cool, and this book is all about learning how to be a 21st century magician. I will take you on a journey from knowing nothing about magic to becoming a skilled magician, ready to perform tricks at a moment's notice.

However, if you want to be a COOL magician, learning the tricks is just part of the ride. Although the tricks and their methods are important, you need to engage with your audience, too. That's the real secret of magic. The good news is that it's not too tricky to learn and this book will guide you through the process, taking you from zero to hero.

When I first started performing magic, I was shy, nervous and worried about whether a trick would work, or if people would even like my magic. But with a little hard work and dedication, I started to get amazing results. Now I've been on stage in front of audiences of 2000 people and have created YouTube videos that have been watched by people all over the world.

Magic is a gift that keeps on giving – once you've mastered it, you can pass on that feeling of wonder to other people. If you treat magic in this way, you'll become a TRUE magician.

# BUILD YOUR ACT

Are you ready to put on a magic show? The first step is for you to choose the type of magician you want to be and to learn some amazing magic that fits that style. Whether it's a quick, spontaneous show for your friends in between classes, an after-dinner show for your family or a full-on stage show in front of a big audience, you'll need a bag of tricks. Doing one trick is cool and two tricks is intriguing, but performing three tricks in front of an excited audience shows you have what it takes to become a master magician. This book will guide you through the steps you need to take to build your act and put on a spectacular magic show.

### CHOOSE A STYLE

Which types of magic do you like?
What kind of magician will you be?

### CHOOSE THREE TRICKS

Choose an opener, a middle and a finale trick that fit your theme.

### STRUCTURE YOUR SHOW

Does your show have a story?
Do you have a script?

### PLAN YOUR STAGING

Where will you perform?
What will you wear?

### REHEARSE

Go over each part of the trick to make sure it works.

### PROMOTE YOUR SHOW

Check out some great ideas to get people excited about your magic show.

# MAGICIAN'S CODE

**Before you start learning tricks, it's important to first understand the magician's code. This can be broken down into three simple rules, which will help you to be the best magician you can be.**

### 1. NEVER REVEAL THE SECRET OF A TRICK

People always wonder why magicians are so protective of their secrets. The truth is, the magician wants to keep that sense of magic and wonder an audience gets when they first see a trick. Once the audience knows how a trick is done, they aren't amazed by it anymore.

### 2. DON'T REPEAT A TRICK FOR THE SAME AUDIENCE

Many magic tricks rely on an element of surprise to amaze the audience. If the audience knows what to expect, they'll be looking for anything that reveals how the magician did the impossible. This could spoil that sense of magic.

### 3. PRACTISE, PRACTISE, PRACTISE

How you practise is just as important as how often you practise. When it comes to learning new sleights, repetition is key, so you get a feeling for how your props move. You also need to develop muscle memory in your hands, so you can do the sleights almost without thinking about them.

# MAKING OLD TRICKS NEW

**There's a saying that you can't teach an old dog new tricks, but with magic you can take old tricks and make them look brand new!**

## MODERN MAGIC

Modern magic is where you take things that we use in our everyday lives and do extraordinary things with them, such as making a coin disappear. Some people call this street magic, but this style of magic can be seen everywhere nowadays, from the street to the stage.

Modern magic can really wow your audience because spectators recognise the items as ordinary and know that what they are witnessing should be impossible. It gives you, the magician, extra power because of the assumptions your audience makes about the items you are using.

## OLD SCHOOL CAN BE COOL

Magic is an old type of entertainment. Magicians have been coming up with clever ways to surprise and fool audiences for thousands of years. So much great magic already exists, but for 21st century magicians, the challenge is to come up with exciting new tricks as well as finding ways to make old tricks look cool.

## ADD A TWIST

The tricks in this book are based on some old classic tricks but have been brought up to date. One of the ways this has been done is to use modern magic and substitute traditional props for objects we use today. For example, you could use cards from your favourite board game instead of a deck of cards. The tricks in this book also feature smartphones and technology to give them a modern twist.

# HOW DO YOU LIKE YOUR MAGIC?

**Do you want to do magic anytime, anywhere? Or put on a spectacular show for your family and friends? Performing magic can be broken down into different styles or themes. Read the descriptions and think about how you might like to perform your tricks.**

## STREET

Street magic was first made popular on television by the incredible magician David Blaine. Street magic is any type of magic that is performed in a casual setting, such as on the street or in the school canteen. Usually the props are everyday items – for example, you borrow things from your audience. This makes for a stronger reaction, because not only were your audience not expecting to be amazed, but you amazed them with their own stuff!

## STAGE

Stage magic is done on stage in front of an audience. Usually a stage act has a theme, and the costume and set design match this theme. The magic may be performed to music, have a script and include audience participation.

## PARLOUR

Parlour magic is a show that is performed in front of an audience of up to 80 people. The magician may be on the same level as the audience, instead of on a stage. The tricks are smaller than those in a stage show, and since they are closer to the magic, the audience feels more involved.

## IMPROMPTU

Impromptu magic happens off the cuff with no obvious set up (even if you, as the magician, are secretly prepared and ready to do a trick). Like street magic, the tricks are done with ordinary things. Impromptu magic is usually the strongest type of magic because of the shock factor in seeing something completely astonishing without any warning. An example would be making a pen vanish into thin air.

## MIND READING

In this book, mind-reading magic is where you either correctly guess what a spectator is thinking or you predict something that will happen in the future, such as a particular playing card being selected by the audience.

## CLOSE-UP

Close-up magic is when the audience is right next to you. People are so close to the magic that they cannot believe their eyes. Close-up magic tricks include those that are done in spectators' hands or on a table.

# GET IT RIGHT!

**A rehearsal gives you an idea of timing, and highlights any things that might go wrong. To make sure you get it right, it can help to run through your show before you perform. This will make you feel much more comfortable when it comes to actually doing the show!**

### TAKE THE STAGE

If you're putting on a proper show, try to find time to rehearse in the space you'll be performing in. Map out where to place your props, where to stand and where your spectators will be if they come up to help with a trick. If it isn't possible to get into the actual space, try to get hold of some photos so you visualise it, try to picture where everything can go and set it up somewhere else.

### ALL DRESSED UP!

Do a complete dress rehearsal. Lay out all of your props, put on the clothes you will wear and do the tricks to a pretend audience. Talk out loud to an imaginary audience as if they were sitting in front of you and make up names for fake people as you ask them to help with the trick. This tip will help you understand the flow of your show and how long each trick takes.

### FILM EVIDENCE

Film yourself practising from different angles. When you look back at the footage, you'll see how your magic really looks. The beauty of the camera is that it captures everything – it's your best friend when it comes to telling you what you do well and what needs work. You may not like what you see at first but it's one of the fastest ways of getting better!

**TIP**

Be wary of practising in front of a mirror. While the trick might look great from one angle, that's only one of many – especially if the audience is surrounding you, they'll be seeing the trick from all sides.

# WHICH TRICKS SUIT YOUR SHOW?

**Now it's time to choose some awesome tricks. Choose an opener, a middle and a finale trick that fit together and work well with your theme. Here are some trick suggestions for different themes.**

## IMPROMPTU THEME

Quick, straightforward tricks using everyday objects work well for an impromptu magic show.

**TOP TRICK CHOICES:**

Pen and Coin Flurry p56
Vanishing Pen p52
Band Link p54

## MIND READING THEME

This will have more impact if you just concentrate on one or two areas. You could become an expert at body language, predict the future, or hone your psychic abilities.

**TOP TRICK CHOICES:**

Watch Hands Prediction p86
Multiple Outs p76
Photo Prediction p90

## INTERACTIVE THEME

For this type of magic show, you could invite spectators on the stage to help you. This can provide some comedy as you interact with them on stage.

**TOP TRICK CHOICES:**

Body Illusion p50
Coin to Impossible Location p100
Ziplock Force Bag p96

## TECH THEME

You might want to combine your magic tricks with tech and twist your audience's perception of what magic can be. For example, use phones to make predictions, pull photos out of phones or become a lie detector.

**TOP TRICK CHOICES:**

Photo Prediction p90
3D Printer Phone p22
Ziplock Force Bag p96

# MAKE YOUR TRICKS UNIQUE

**To make your show interesting, it's important to put your own stamp on it. Here are some ideas for making the tricks your own.**

It's a case of taking your hobbies (aside from magic!) and using them as creative inspiration for the 'story' of each trick. For example, if you like to go running, you could introduce the cut and restored shoelace trick on page 60 by saying how you tripped up on an untied shoelace one day and then wished you could magically repair it.

Make a list of 10 things you like and 10 tricks from this book. Then randomly connect them to create a story that fits the trick. Look at this table for some examples.

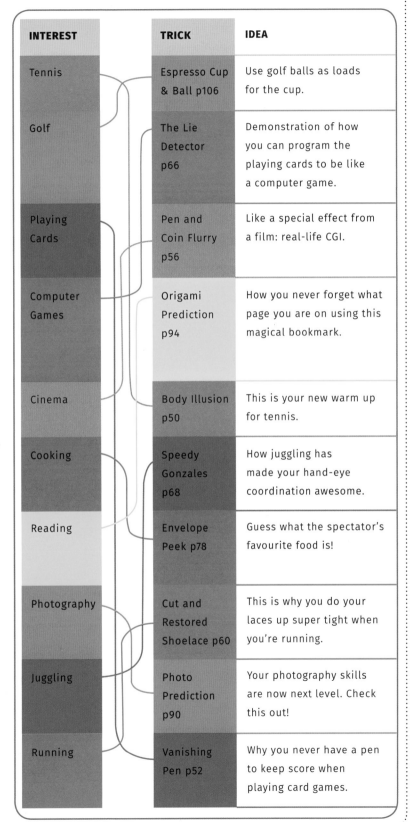

| INTEREST | TRICK | IDEA |
|----------|-------|------|
| Tennis | Espresso Cup & Ball p106 | Use golf balls as loads for the cup. |
| Golf | The Lie Detector p66 | Demonstration of how you can program the playing cards to be like a computer game. |
| Playing Cards | Pen and Coin Flurry p56 | Like a special effect from a film: real-life CGI. |
| Computer Games | Origami Prediction p94 | How you never forget what page you are on using this magical bookmark. |
| Cinema | Body Illusion p50 | This is your new warm up for tennis. |
| Cooking | Speedy Gonzales p68 | How juggling has made your hand-eye coordination awesome. |
| Reading | Envelope Peek p78 | Guess what the spectator's favourite food is! |
| Photography | Cut and Restored Shoelace p60 | This is why you do your laces up super tight when you're running. |
| Juggling | Photo Prediction p90 | Your photography skills are now next level. Check this out! |
| Running | Vanishing Pen p52 | Why you never have a pen to keep score when playing card games. |

# STRUCTURING YOUR SHOW

**Once you've chosen the type of magic and the tricks you want to perform, it's time to put it all together and think about the structure of your show.**

### WHAT'S THE STORY?

Structure is all about theme and boils down to one word... story. What is the story around your show? It could be as simple as a few sentences or a single fact that captures the audience's attention at the start of your show.

If you've chosen a mind reading theme, you could talk briefly about the history of clairvoyants and how you've been studying their skills to create a show unlike anything seen before.

If you've chosen an interactive theme, you could introduce the Espresso Cup and Ball trick (see page 106) by saying that it used to be a con game and then invite someone to play the game with you. You could then do a trick about card cheating, to continue the con game theme.

# SUPER SCRIPT

**Practise a trick to get a feel for where the high points (the exciting bits) and the low points are, to work out where there's space to talk. The more you perform a trick, the more you'll get a feel for what to say and when.**

## TIME TO TALK

Some tricks are so quick or visual that they don't need a big introduction. Sometimes it's best to let the magic speak for itself! But if you're doing more of a show, having something to say along with the magic makes the whole experience more entertaining.

Here are some examples of stories that you could tell through your magic...

This is the trick that fooled Houdini...

Normally I only show this trick to my magician friends but...

I'm going to break a rule of magic and...

Wouldn't it be cool if you could predict the lottery?

This trick took me a year to learn...

What if you could tell what someone else is thinking?

What if you could cheat at cards?

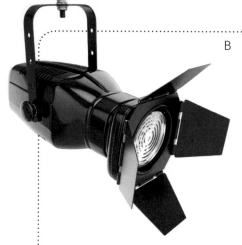

# TAKE THE STAGE

**To put on a big show, you need to think about your show's staging – what and where you want everything on stage. This includes your props and the people who come on stage to help you with the tricks!**

1. Decide on the order in which you will do each trick. Record them on a **crib sheet**.

2. Make a list of the items you need to perform each trick. You might need a table to put the props on, or you could just put them in your pockets if they fit.

3. If someone comes on stage to help you, do you want them on your left or right? You don't want to keep walking past them to get things – keep it slick. And make sure they can't see part of the method from where they stand.

4. Think about the seating of your audience. You want everyone to have a good view of the magic. Will your audience be seated or standing, in a semi-circle or in rows? You want it to be easy for people to get out of their seats and quickly come up on stage to help.

5. Practise your complete magic show on stage. Do **dry rehearsals**, which are performed without an audience, and **dress rehearsals** in full costume with an audience.

# WHAT TO WEAR

**What you wear when you perform is an important part of your stage presence and says a lot about you as a performer.**

## CHOOSE CAREFULLY

If you're dressed smartly, people will expect a certain style of magic (most likely parlour or stage). Whereas if you're dressed casually, it might be more surprising for your audience if they see something amazing.

Remember that for certain tricks, you might need your clothes to have room for props, so go for something with pockets and wide sleeves. Your clothes can also be part of the story of your magic show.

## BE COMFY!

It's important to be comfortable with what you're wearing when performing magic. You have enough things to think about without feeling awkward!

### HERE ARE SOME IDEAS...

- School uniform
- Jeans and t-shirt
- A smart suit
- Fancy dress
- Something sparkly!

# MARKETING YOURSELF

**Although your tricks need to be amazing, it's the way you perform them and deal with people that really counts. You are the magic – the tricks are secondary!**

### SHOW YOUR FRIENDS

If you're going to market yourself as a magician, first you'll need to amaze your friends with your tricks. Then, with any luck, your friends will spread the word – and other people will want to see your magic, too.

### GET YOURSELF ONLINE

Create your own YouTube channel, Facebook page or Instagram feed dedicated to your new magician skills. Look at other magicians you like, and use their style for inspiration, adding your own twist.

### SHOWCASE YOUR SKILLS

To launch your social media presence, it can really help to create a video that not only shows your incredible skills and style, but also captures the amazing reactions of your audiences. With a little thought and help from a friend to hold the camera, you can capture some awesome footage that will let people know what you're all about.

### SPREAD THE MAGIC

It's much easier today to 'spread the magic' on social media and to share content digitally. To wow your fans, try filming new tricks you've learnt and upload videos and photos of your shows.

### TOP TIPS

1. Know your tricks before filming.

2. Try to post regularly on social media, but make sure it's always something new and exciting!

3. Research, 'like' and 'follow' other magicians, and see if there's a young magicians' group near you.

4. Share details of where and when people can see you perform next.

5. Do your best to stay dedicated and committed, so you have a strong, steady online presence!

# THE MAGIC OF FILMING

**Filming magic is a great way to get your work out there in front of people. Here are some handy filming tips.**

### NOT A GOOD LOOK

Some tricks look better on camera than others (see the Magic Tricks for Social Media section). Tricks that rely on the element of surprise – such as the Envelope and Coins Prediction Trick on page 104 – will not work on camera. People will be surprised the first time they see it, but they'll be able to re-watch the video and see the secret.

### ASK A FRIEND

It's great if a friend can film you because they can tell you how you look through the camera lens. And it's really useful to have someone to press record and hit pause!

### THE BEST OF THE BUNCH

Always film a trick a number of times. Then check your footage and decide which take is best.

### WHAT EQUIPMENT DO I NEED?

The camera on a mobile phone is powerful enough to use for filming magic. You can set it up on a tripod to keep it steady and make the footage look professional. However, if you're filming street magic then it helps to have a friend with a steady hand!

### MIX IT UP!

When filming a whole routine, film it with two different groups of spectators in separate locations. When you edit the video, you can cut between the groups to give the video more variety. Plus, you can edit out the boring bits and any parts that might give away the trick.

**TIP**

Some tricks will need one continuous film so your viewers know you didn't do any camera tricks.

# PR STUNTS FOR YOUR SHOW

**A PR stunt is something big and bold that attracts attention to you and your magic. It's all about creating a buzz to make people want to see you!**

### GUERILLA MARKETING

If you are doing a show, it could be cool to post a prediction to the address where your show will be held or to the person who has booked your show. Post it way ahead of time and mark the letter: Do not open until the date of the show. It could contain a prediction about one of your tricks, maybe a selected playing card or the correctly predicted number printed out.

### SECRET MESSAGES

People love a bit of mystery. If you can, write a cryptic message on the whiteboard in class – something that will make your classmates wonder about your magical powers. You could write, "You will choose the seven of diamonds." Or: "I know what you are thinking!"

### THE HOUDINI CHALK IDEA

Harry Houdini was famous for rolling into towns with his show and creating huge publicity. His assistants would run ahead writing on the pavements in chalk, directing people to the box office to buy tickets. You could do something similar directing people to your magic.

TIP

1. Get your friends to video you doing a cool trick and tell them to share it with their friends. If they tag you, then other people will start to follow you.

**TIP**

2. Post one video magic trick each day during the week running up to your show. See page 17 for some filming tips.

**TIP**

3. Go Live! Use the power of social media live video to tell your friends, family and fans when you are next planning on doing magic.

**TIP**

4. If you know someone with a large following, perform some amazing magic on them and ask them to share it on their channels and tag you in the post. This will get your magic out to a much bigger audience.

**TIP**

5. Create your own HASHTAG. Once you have astounded people with your magic, ask them to post a photo about the experience and get them to use your hashtag.

These camera-style tricks make cool videos. They will help boost your social media presence and help spread the word about what an awesome magician you are.

# MAGIC TRICKS FOR SOCIAL MEDIA

# 3D PRINTER PHONE

## You Will Need:

- everyday object
- mobile phone

**Magically print an ordinary object from the screen of your mobile phone.**

1 Beforehand, take two photos on your phone with exactly the same background. Show the object in one photo, but make sure it's missing from the other.

2 Store the photos in a separate album where you can access them quickly.

3 **Finger palm** (see page 32) the object and hold it out of sight at the back of your phone while displaying the photo of the object on your phone to the audience.

4 Then scroll your phone and slide onto the next blank background photo. As you do this, pull the actual object out from the back of the phone. With good timing it will really look like you pull the object from the screen!

# MAGIC MAKES MONEY

## You Will Need:

- two banknotes
- one playing card
- glue

## Change a banknote into a playing card in an instant.

**2** To perform the trick, pinch the folded notes with your first finger and thumb. Hold the card facing front with your second finger. With a flick forwards, release the card, holding on to the notes tightly. The card will fall forward and the audience will see the note 'appear'.

**3** With your other hand, run your thumb down the back of the second note, carefully unfolding it so it is square with the visible note.

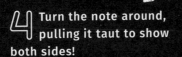

**1** Glue the card to one end of the first note, making sure the edges line up. At the other end of the note attach a second note that matches the orientation of the first. Fold the notes as shown.

**4** Turn the note around, pulling it taut to show both sides!

# PHONE IN A BOTTLE

## You Will Need:

- empty plastic bottle
- craft knife
- mobile phone

Slam a mobile phone through the side of an empty plastic bottle.

TIP
Do this trick over a soft surface to avoid breakages!

1 Carefully cut a slit into the side of an empty plastic bottle that is big enough to hold your mobile phone inside.

2 To perform the trick, simply slam the phone through the slit. From the front it will look like the phone went through the bottle!

Ask an adult to help you cut the drinks bottle.

# SNAP CHANGE

## You Will Need:

- one playing card
- one credit card or loyalty card

## With a snap of your fingers, instantly change a playing card into a credit card.

**1** Line up the two cards so the smaller plastic card is hidden behind the playing card.

**2** Pinch the cards together with your first, second finger and thumb as shown.

**3** To change the cards, pull back with your second finger, pulling the card at the front backwards towards the base of your thumb.

**4** The card is clipped between your second finger and the base of your thumb. It will stay hidden behind the card the audience can see. This card is pinched now with just your thumb and first finger.

**TIP**
Practise this move until you can do it smoothly and quickly.

# RING TO KEY

## You Will Need:

- one ring
- one door key
- double-sided tape

With a wave of their hand, the magician magically changes an ordinary ring into a door key.

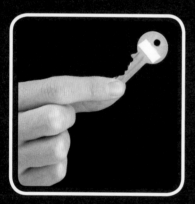

**1** Beforehand, place some double-sided sticky tape on the back of the key as shown.

**2** For the trick, **finger palm** (see page 32) the key in your right hand.

**3** Then hold up the ring with your left hand, in your first finger and thumb.

**4** Bring your right hand in front of the ring. Line them up so the base of the key covers the ring.

**5** Push the ring and the key together to stick the ring to the key. Make sure that you don't reveal the key from the front yet! Keep it covered with the first and second fingers on each hand.

**6** Make a magical gesture and reveal the key instead of the ring.

**7** Show your hands are empty, too. The ring has vanished! It's an awesome illusion as the hole in the key can still be seen through, even though the ring is hidden behind!

# COLOUR CHANGE

## You Will Need:

- one deck of cards

**With a magical pass of their hand, the magician changes one playing card as quick as lightning for another.**

2 Move your other hand so your palm touches the bottom edge of the bottom card. The rest of the hand is raised up slightly to make the illusion real.

3 As you touch the bottom card, press downwards and onto the deck. Pop the card off the deck at an angle. Keep your fingers apart and the second from bottom card will look like it magically appeared.

1 Place two contrasting cards at the bottom of a deck – for example, the Queen of Hearts and the Ace of Clubs. Then hold the cards face up in **dealer's grip.**

**4** To change the card back, smoothly move your hand back over the other hand with the card. Then square the deck.

**TIP**

Use the bottom edge of the deck as a pivot point and anchor for the bottom card to keep it hidden in your palm.

# CARD TRICK BASICS

Now it's time to learn some basics. Practise these basic card trick moves first, before you go on to the tricks.

### FINGER BREAK

Use your little finger to keep a gap between the two packets of cards to mark the location of a particular card. With the right grip pressure, the break cannot be seen from the front of the deck.

### THUMB BREAK

The pad of your thumb keeps a break between the two halves of the deck while in a grip called a biddle grip.

### RIFFLE FORCE

The force card starts on top of the deck. Cut the cards and keep a little finger break above the force card. Run your thumb down the side of the deck and ask the spectator to call 'stop'. Try to time it so they stop somewhere near the middle of the pack. No matter where they say stop, cut the cards at your 'break' and hand them the force card.

## PALMING

1 Obtain a break under the card or cards to be palmed.

2 Insert your third finger into the break and extend it, shooting the card into your palm.

## RIFFLE SHUFFLE

Split the deck into two even piles. Line them up, then flick them to blend the two piles together.

## OVER HAND SHUFFLE

1 Holding the cards as shown, run the cards from your right hand to your left hand using your left thumb to pull them down one or a few at a time.

2 An **injog** is where you pull one card inwards closer to your body to mark its position. It can then be pulled up to create a break as the cards are squared and held in dealer's grip.

## CONCERTINA SHUFFLE

Split the cards into two even piles. Twist the cards and then push them together.

# COIN TRICK BASICS

**Master these basic techniques to become a coin trick master.**

## CLASSIC PALM

This is a method for hiding a coin in the palm of your hand.

Find the sweet spot and practise keeping the coin there for a while. Once you can extend and move your fingers freely, you've really nailed it!

## FINGER PALM

1 This is a more relaxed method of hiding a coin. Your fingers should curl naturally as the coin rests against them.

2 To produce a coin from a finger palm hold, tip your hand downwards so gravity allows your thumb to slip it out to the fingertips.

## BOBO'S COIN SWITCH

**1** Hold the hidden coin in a finger palm and the other coin, which your audience can see, in your fingertips.

**2** As you pretend to throw down the visible coin, you actually let go of the palmed coin and slide the visible coin in its place, into a finger palm.

## FRENCH DROP

 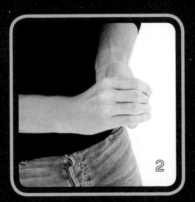 

 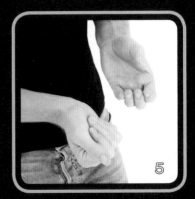

Display the coin between your fingers and thumb. Pretend to take the coin into your other hand but allow it to drop into finger palm. The deceptive part is the space left between your fingers and thumb. The audience will assume it is in your other closed hand and you are able to make the coin vanish.

# MIND-READING BASICS

**Two types of mind-reading tricks are covered in this book: predicting something that will happen in the future and plucking a thought from the mind of someone in the audience.**

## MEMORY EXERCISE

Memory plays a big part in many mind-reading tricks. This is a useful exercise that you can use to help you remember things in your mind reading magic show.

Memorise this list – you'll notice each object rhymes with the number! Once you know it off by heart, it can help you remember any list of 10 things.

| | |
|---|---|
| 1 Bun | 6 Sticks |
| 2 Shoe | 7 Heaven |
| 3 Tree | 8 Plate |
| 4 Door | 9 Line |
| 5 Hive | 10 Hen |

During your show, ask volunteers to call out random objects. As each object is called out, try to create a picture in your mind that will link the object to its place on the list.

For example, if the first object called out is an elephant, picture an elephant biting into a huge iced bun (because bun is number one on your special list that helps you memorise things).

If the second object is a window, imagine the window of a shoe shop – or better still, funny little windows on a shoe-shaped house.

The crazier and more visual the connection you make, the easier it will be to remember. With practice, you'll be able to memorise any list within about 20 seconds.

To make mind reading appear genuine, it's a good idea to create a character for yourself to show off your amazing tricks. Here are some ideas for characters. How would you do the trick if you were…

**Telepathic**: could read someone's thoughts.

**Body Language Expert**: could read someone's body language.

**Human Lie Detector:** could know if someone is telling lies.

**Remote Viewer:** could sense a thing, person or place from a long way away.

**Hypnotist**: could put a person in a trance and affect their behaviour.

**Psychokinetic:** could move objects with your mind.

**Clairvoyant:** had the power to see the future.

Your answers to the above will determine the strength, believability and impact of your routines.

# A MAGICIAN'S TOOLS

**A magician's tools are the skills and techniques you will use to take your magic to the next level.**

### SLEIGHT OF HAND

The fancy fingerwork such as palming a coin, controlling a chosen card or even using your memory! Good **sleight of hand** should be invisible or at least look like a normal action.

### GIMMICKS

Gimmicks are specially-made objects that look ordinary, but have special features used in magic tricks. The audience doesn't know that the object is specially made.

### MOTIVATED ACTIONS

If you've just vanished an object and you need to ditch it without the audience knowing, all you need is a reason for reaching into your pocket. Perhaps you have a pen there, which you need for the next trick. So, as you get the pen from your pocket, you secretly ditch the vanished object at the same time and the audience doesn't notice.

# TYPES OF MISDIRECTION

This is the way that you control your audience's attention during your magic show so they don't spot how a trick is done. A good magician can **misdirect** an audience's attention in many ways.

## PHYSICAL

A brilliant rule of magic is that a bigger action covers a smaller action. In the appearing coin trick on page 59, as your hand waves around your other closed fist (big action), nobody sees the coin fall into your fist (small action).

## LAUGHTER

When people laugh they relax, so this is a great moment to do something sneaky to make your trick work.

## VERBAL

Ask your audience a question. While they think about the answer, they're not paying much attention to what you're doing.

## EYE CONTACT

Your audience look where you look. So if you make eye contact with them as you do a sleight, they're less likely to be watching your hands.

## ON AND OFF BEATS

There are highs and lows during a trick that create attention and relaxation in your audience. If you look like you're focused on something, your audience will focus on it, too.

## BODY LANGUAGE

Your body language plays a huge role in misdirecting the audience's attention. Look at how other magicians make something seem interesting or not with their posture and facial expression. Which type of movement gives them the best opportunity to do something sneaky?

# TROUBLESHOOTING

**If a trick goes wrong, it's usually because you haven't practised enough and you're not quite ready to perform it.**

### HOW DO YOU KNOW WHEN YOU'RE READY?

This is a tricky one. Honestly, just taking the plunge and attempting the trick for an audience after solid practice is a good idea. You'll know then if it was ready. Eventually you'll develop a feel for when a trick is ready for action.

### "I SAW HOW YOU DID THAT!"

If someone says they saw how you did a trick don't get frustrated with them. If anything, you should be thanking them for the opportunity to make your magic even better!

### FLASHES

A flash is when the magician accidentally exposes part of the method for a trick, for example by flashing a coin that is hidden in classic palm.

## SLEIGHT OF HAND

Sleight of hand is important in loads of tricks. Learning the move takes time and can be frustrating. But once you have mastered a sleight, it's an awesome feeling. Here are some tips to help with your learning…

1. When first attempting a sleight, try to copy the steps in this book – especially the hand movements – as closely as possible. This will help you learn the sleight the right way from the start.

2. Do each part of the sleight slowly at the beginning. This will help your body gain muscle memory for the correct way of doing something. And it will help you with timing actions.

3. Practise how the movement would look if you weren't doing sleight of hand. This technique is known as the Vernon touch. You want your sleight of hand to look natural, like the real thing.

4. Learn new sleights in stages. You won't always be able to move smoothly onto the next part straight away. Sometimes you'll get stuck for ages, and then all of a sudden be able to do the whole sleight – or at least part of it. That's okay, and to be expected.

5. If you've been practising for ages and are struggling to get it right, take a break and come back to it fresh.

# TIPS

Now you know the basics and have some magic weapons up your sleeve.  All you need now are some top tips to polish your act and turn you into a master magician.

### BE FLEXIBLE

Unexpected things happen and could easily interrupt your show – such as a spectator arriving late, or dropping or knocking something over on stage. As a magician, you need to be flexible. Preparing for these unexpected events will make your audience feel they are in expert hands and they will relax.

### LET THE SETTING DICTATE THE MAGIC

If you're at the dinner table entertaining your family, it would be cool to be ready with some magic that uses the cutlery and perhaps a deck of cards that is close by. Or if you're out with friends in the park, you could use some of the coins they have in their pockets and maybe one of their mobile phones to make magic happen.

## ALWAYS BE READY

When you tell somebody that you're a magician, usually the next thing they will say is… "Can you show me a trick?" So it's smart to always be prepared and have a few impromptu tricks up your sleeve.

## AVOID NARRATING YOUR TRICKS

A magic show is a show, not a tell! That means your audience are watching exactly what you are doing, so you don't need to describe it to them. For example, don't say, "I am going to shuffle your card back into the pack." It's boring and may draw attention to parts of your magic method that you don't want to reveal.

## YOUR ATTENTION PLEASE

Your audience will pay attention to whatever you're paying attention to. If you're staring at your hands as you do a **sleight**, the audience will too – and then they might see how you're doing it!

## THE POWER OF THREE IS STRONG

In a book, a film or a magic show, we crave a beginning, a middle and an ending. Grouping things in three is more satisfying to your audience. That is why the tricks in this book are divided into openers, middles and finales. **So creating your show is as easy as 1, 2, 3!**

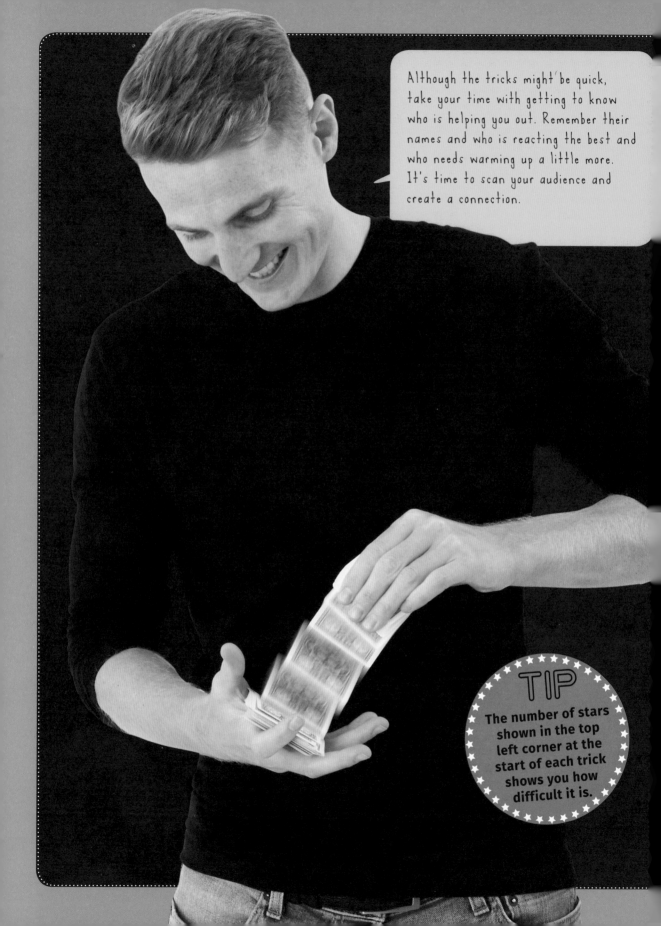

Although the tricks might be quick, take your time with getting to know who is helping you out. Remember their names and who is reacting the best and who needs warming up a little more. It's time to scan your audience and create a connection.

TIP
The number of stars shown in the top left corner at the start of each trick shows you how difficult it is.

These opening tricks help to capture your audience's attention and make them want to see more. The tricks are quick, slick and really magical. They need little preparation and can be done on the fly.

# OPENERS

# FOUR ACE PRODUCTION

## You Will Need:

- one deck of cards

**Magically produce the four aces one by one from a shuffled pack of cards.**

1 Beforehand stack the deck so the four aces are on top in the following order... Ace of Clubs, random card, Ace of Diamonds, Ace of Spades, Ace of Hearts, rest of deck.

2 Give the cards a **riffle shuffle**, making sure to keep the top five cards unaltered on top of the deck.

3 Pretend to **cut** the cards to reveal the first ace. But actually use the following false cut and turn over the top card.

4 Hold the deck in **dealer's grip**, cut off a third of the deck and place it on the table, then cut off another third and place this next to the first. Finally put the rest of the deck down next to the second pile.

**5** Put the first pile on top of the second. Then put this larger pile on top of the third pile. As you do this turn over the top card to reveal the Ace of Clubs.

**6** Do a **slip cut** to reveal the second ace, the Ace of Diamonds. Pick up the cards in **dealer's grip**, and with your thumb and second finger of your other hand, pull up on about half the deck. As you do this the thumb that is resting on the deck draws back the top card onto the bottom half.

**7** Pick up the top half and slap it down onto the other half. Turn over the new top card to reveal the Ace of Diamonds.

**9** As the cards square up, cut the remainder of the cards below the thumb break to the new top of the deck. This secretly brings one ace to the bottom of the deck and keeps one ace on top.

**8** Hold the deck in dealer's grip, with your right thumb, gently pull up on the top card and keep a little gap between that card and the top of the deck. This is called a **thumb break**. Let half of the deck fall into your left hand in dealer's grip and cut those to the top of the deck.

**10** To produce the last two aces, pinch the deck between your thumb on top and fingers on the bottom. As you toss the cards in your other hand, the two aces will stay trapped in your fingers and thumb. Now reveal the final aces.

# ONE PHASE AMBITIOUS CARD

## You Will Need:

- one deck of cards

**Magically vanish a chosen card from one spectator's pile of cards into another spectator's hands.**

1 Ask a volunteer to sign a card. As you do this, hold the cards in your left hand and pull down the bottom card with your little finger to keep a break.

2 Next hold the cards with your right hand in **biddle grip**, and transfer the break to your thumb.

3 Swing cut half of the cards into your right hand. Take back the chosen card and use the right hand packet to flip the chosen card face down.

4 Use the tips of your right first and second fingers to push the chosen card forwards about halfway, keeping the rest of the cards square.

**5** Use the left third finger and little finger to grab the card that you have been holding in thumb break. As you grab the card, turn over the left hand packet to show the chosen card.

**6** Now with the base of the right hand packet, push the chosen card square with the left hand packet.

**7** Make a fan of the cards with your right hand. Then use your left hand to **thumb off** the top card and push it into the fan.

**8** Ask someone on your right to push the card in all the way, as you give the left hand packet to someone else. Your attention is on the right hand packet. Give it to someone else once the card has been pushed in.

**9** Now tell the audience that the chosen card will vanish from one pile... snap, and it's gone. Ask them to spread through the cards to look for it.

**10** Make a magical gesture towards the forgotten left pile and ask a spectator to turn over the top card to reveal the chosen card!

# PULSE READING

## You Will Need:

- one deck of cards

Using your magical skills, read the subtle changes in a spectator's heart rate to detect a freely chosen card.

1 Ask a spectator to shuffle a deck of cards and choose a card.

2 While the spectator shows the card to the audience, turn your back so you don't see the card, but secretly peek at the bottom card of the deck and remember it. This will be your **key card**.

3 Start to **cut** small piles from the top of the deck onto a table and ask the audience to call out 'stop!'

**4** When they do, ask the spectator to place their card onto that pile and then put the rest of the cards on top. This secretly places the chosen card below the key card in the deck.

**5** You want the audience to think that you couldn't possibly know where the chosen card is. So turn around and ask the spectator to cut and complete the deck off centre, as it's maybe around the middle.

**6** Now take the cards and spread them face up on the table.

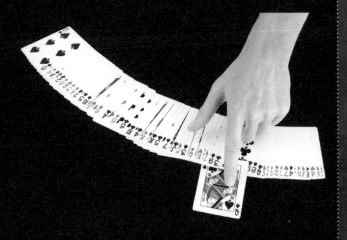

**TIP**

Try to make the audience really believe that you are picking up on pulse signals to find the chosen card.

**8** You are really looking for the key card and the chosen card will be the card to the right of it.

**7** Ask the spectator to hold out their wrist and pretend to feel for small variations in their pulse as you scan your other hand over the cards.

# BODY ILLUSION

## You Will Need:
- Just your hands and the audience's!

Ask the audience to copy your movements – they'll get in a twist, but you'll be magically double-jointed!

**1** Ask the audience to copy your actions. Hold out both hands in front of you and turn them thumbs down.

**2** Put your right hand over your left and interlock your fingers.

**3** Wiggle your thumbs. Ask the audience to do the same… that's easy!

**4** Next ask them to try something more difficult and move the second finger on their right hand. As they are attempting this, take your hands apart and point to someone in the audience with your right hand. Say that they're doing a good job and well done.

**5** When you bring your hands back together, this time secretly put your right hand underneath your left. Twist it the other way and once again interlock your fingers.

**6** Ask the audience to copy you on the count of three… twist your arms anti-clockwise so your thumbs are pointing upwards. The audience will not be able to do this and leave themselves in a twist.

# VANISHING PEN

## You Will Need:

- a pen with a lid
- a rubber band
- scissors
- a safety pin
- glue
- a jacket

**Take a pen from your pocket and magically vanish it into thin air.**

1 To make a **gimmick** called a **pull,** cut a large long rubber band so you have a long strand of elastic. Attach one end to a safety pin and carefully tie the other end to the cap of the pen.

2 Attach the safety pin to the inside of your jacket.

3 Put your jacket on and place the pen in your inside pocket. You can glue the lid of the pen onto the pen to make it more secure.

4 In front of your audience, take the pen out of your pocket, making sure that the elastic stays hidden. Say that you are going to make the pen vanish into thin air.

5 With a magical gesture and some physical **misdirection**, let the pen shoot back inside your jacket and show your hands empty.

# BAND LINK

## You Will Need:

- two rubber bands

## Impossibly link together two ordinary elastic bands.

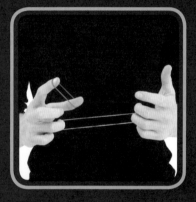

**1** Hold one rubber band between your right first finger and thumb. Hold the other rubber band between your two third fingers.

**2** Push your right thumb through the middle of the lower band and use your left first finger to hook the right band in the middle.

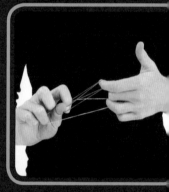

**3** Now insert your right first finger into the lower two strands of the right band near your right thumb.

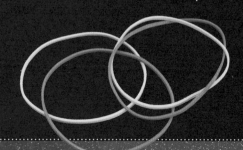

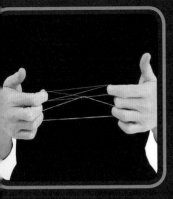

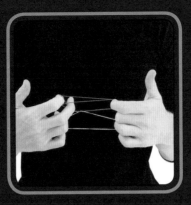

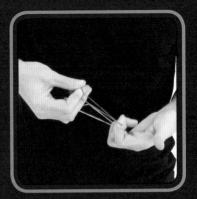

**4** Carefully release the strands off of the right thumb onto the right first finger to create a figure of 8 with the upper band around the lower band.

**5** Now take your right second finger and insert it from the front to the furthest left part of the upper band. Stretch the finger and band back to the right so the right first and second fingers are next to each other.

**6** Roll the strands off of the right first finger to the back of the top joint of the second finger with your right thumb. This movement links the bands and holds them together.

**8** Let the lower band drop to show the magically linked rubber bands.

**7** Insert your left second finger in place of the first finger to mirror the right hand.

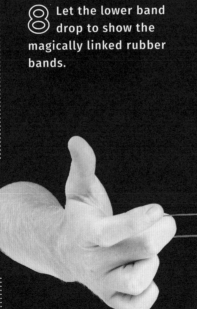

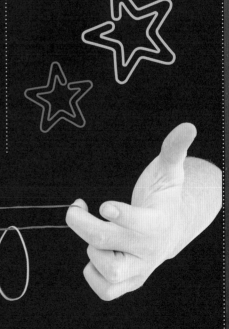

# PEN AND COIN FLURRY

## You Will Need:

- a pen
- a coin
  (both a comfortable size for your hands)

Use a pen to make a coin vanish and reappear, then make the pen and coin magically change places!

**1** Show a pen in your left hand and a coin in your right hand to the audience. Put the pen under your right arm and toss the coin openly into your left hand.

**2** Do a **false transfer** and pretend to throw the coin back into your right hand.

**3** As the coin is palmed in the left hand, the left hand grabs the pen from under the right arm.

### TIP
Time your actions: as you close your right hand around the imaginary coin, your fingers should curl around the coin in the left finger palm.

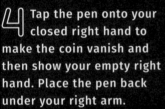

**4** Tap the pen onto your closed right hand to make the coin vanish and then show your empty right hand. Place the pen back under your right arm.

**5** Pretend to pick up an imaginary coin from your right palm. As you do this, drop the coin into your curled right fingers. This is called Ramsay subtlety.

**6** Mime picking the coin up with your left hand. Pretend to toss the coin into the air and catch it in your right hand. Follow its imaginary path with your eyes and the audience will follow too.

**8** Relax your left hand to your side. Slide the coin to your right fingertips to show it has returned.

**10** Take the pen in your left hand. Finally, turn your right hand palm down, press your thumb against the coin and slide the coin along the fingers to the tips, and magically find it from under your arm.

**7** Pick up the pen again in your left hand and tap your closed right hand to make the coin materialise. As you return the pen to your underarm, do a flip stick move and keep the pen hidden in your left hand and mime putting it under your arm.

**9** Bring the left hand in front of the right and let the coin fall into finger palm in the right hand, as you place the pen between your right fingers and thumb. Make a magical gesture with your left hand and show that the pen has appeared.

# APPEARING COIN

## You Will Need:

- a coin that fits the size of your hand

**Show that your hands are empty, and then make a coin appear with a magical gesture.**

Start with a coin hidden in the left hand, in **classic palm**. The audience doesn't know you are holding anything.

*This secret load is called a **Han Ping Chien!***

2 Make a fist with the right hand and move the left hand over to the right in a magical gesture. Drop the coin into the small gap at the top of your closed right hand.

3 Continue to swoop the left hand around the back of the right hand and turn the right hand upwards.

4 Snap the left fingers. Slowly open the right hand to reveal the coin!

# CUT AND RESTORED SHOELACE

## You Will Need:

- two matching shoelaces
- scissors
- two safety pins
- a thick rubber band

Cut a shoelace into two equal lengths with a pair of scissors, and then magically restore them into one piece.

1 Cut one small piece of shoelace as shown in the photo. Attach a small safety pin to the ends of the cut lace and attach that to one end of a thick rubber band.

2 At the other end of the rubber band attach another safety pin and fasten this to the inside of your jacket near the underarm seam.

3 Thread the band and shoelace loop down your sleeve so it is out of sight but just reachable.

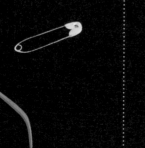

**TIP**

Adjust the safety pin in your jacket so you have just the right amount of tension.

**4** Pretend to make a loop in your left hand. As you do this, secretly grab the **gimmick** shoelace with your right second finger. Pull that into view above your closed left hand instead of the regular shoelace.

**5** Cut the gimmick piece with a pair of scissors, keeping your fist closed so the audience cannot see the extra ends.

**6** As you tuck those cut ends into your fist, allow them to release back up your sleeve via the elastic pull. You will be left with just the regular lace in your sleeve.

**7** Make a magical gesture and show that the lace has been restored! As you open your hand to reveal the lace, it will shoot up your hand.

61

# A SWEET TRICK

## You Will Need:

- one small coin
- a sweet

## A penny magically changes into a sweet!

1 Start with a penny in your left trouser pocket and a sweet in your right pocket. Say to your audience that you are looking for a coin and reach into your pockets at the same time.

2 Bring out the coin and show it at your left fingertips. Keep the sweet **finger palmed** in your right hand.

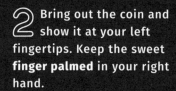

**3** Next perform a sleight called a **shuttle pass**. Toss the coin from your left hand to your right. As you do this, secretly throw the sweet from your right hand into your left. This is a subtle way of hinting to the audience that your hands only contain the penny, without actually showing them empty.

**4** Now throw the sweet from the left finger palm into your right hand. At the same time, finger palm the coin from your right hand into your left. The coin has magically changed into the sweet! This is called a **bobo switch**.

Use your skills to keep the show flowing. A good show has highs and lows to keep the audience on the edge of their seats. Keep that thought in mind as you structure your show. Perhaps use your script to create a climax or a clever moment.

Now you have the audience's attention, are you ready to take the mystery up a notch? These tricks require more concentration but the payoff is well worth it. It's time to really make an impact on your audience and show them how astonishing magic can be!

# MIDDLES

# THE LIE DETECTOR

## You Will Need:

- one deck of cards

## Find an audience member's card by playing a game of true or false.

**1** Ask a spectator to **shuffle** the deck and deal down 9 cards.

**2** Fan the cards and ask the spectator to think of one. Hand them the pile and ask them to **cut** their card to the face and commit it to memory.

**3** Take the cards back face down, making sure you don't look at the chosen card. **Overhand shuffle** the cards, counting off six cards from the top and dumping the rest on top. This secretly locates the chosen card to the third position from the top.

**4** Tell the spectator they can either lie or tell the truth. No matter what their answers are, you will be able to find their card.

5 Ask the spectator the value of the card. Perhaps they lie and say 'a King'. Spell the word K-I-N-G, dealing one card for each letter of the word onto the table. Then drop the rest of the cards on top. If they say 10, spell T-E-N.

6 Now spell the word O-F dealing one card for each letter onto the table and dropping the rest on top.

7 Finally, ask for the suit of the card. Remind the spectator they can lie or tell the truth. It will be either clubs, hearts, spades or diamonds. Whatever they say, for each letter of the word deal one card onto the table and then drop the remaining cards on top. For example, H-E-A-R-T-S.

8 Incredibly their chosen card will now always be fifth from the top. To reveal the chosen card, slowly pick up one card at a time from the tabled pile and place it into your hand. Counting in your head as you go... 1, 2, 3, 4 and 5!

**TIP**

Pretend to be getting a psychic feel for the chosen card. Pause on the fifth card for dramatic effect.

# SPEEDY GONZALES

## You Will Need:

- one deck of cards
- the box that the playing cards came in

Find a chosen card faster than the speed of light, with the cards inside the card box and inside the spectator's pocket.

**1** Ask a spectator to select and remember a card.

**2 Shuffle** the cards from one hand to the other using your thumb to pull off groups of one or two cards at a time. Invite the spectator to return their card face down to the lower pile.

**3** Shuffle off one card onto the chosen card. **Injog** that card towards yourself about a third of the way. Continue shuffling cards onto the injogged card. Eventually dump the rest of the deck on top.

**TIP**

Practise this control with the 'chosen' card face up, so you'll be able to track the card as you shuffle.

**4** Use the left thumb to push against the njogged card and create a 'V' shape. Grip it tightly with the thumb and second finger of your left hand.

**5** Lift up all of the cards apart from a few from the top and begin shuffling until you hit the last card of the upper part of the 'V'.

**6** Dump the rest of the deck on top. You will now have controlled the chosen card to the top of the deck.

**9** Then reach back into their pocket. Slide your thumb or finger against the cutout part of the card box to remove the chosen card from the box in a flash!

**7** Pick up the card box and place the cards nside. As you insert the flap, squeeze the cards and box with your fingers and thumb to bend the top cards of the deck. nsert the flap between the top card and the rest of the deck.

**8** Place the box into the spectator's pocket and show that your hands are empty.

## TIP

Although you could always put the box into your pocket and pull the card out, it's way more impressive to pull it from the pocket of a spectator!

# JUMPING RING

## You Will Need:

- one borrowed finger ring

## A ring jumps from one finger to another in a flash!

**1** Place the ring on the top joint of your second finger. Extend your first and second finger and rest them on the back of the other hand's closed fist.

**2** Pretend to tap your fingers down onto the back of your hand to make the ring jump from finger to finger.

**3** In reality, as you lift up your fingers, you swap your first finger for your third finger by curling your first finger down as you extend your third finger. This is great example of the bigger action covering the smaller action. As they land back onto your other hand, the ring will appear to have jumped onto the other finger.

**TIP**

Don't keep your fingers still for too long on the back of your hand, so the audience can't tell the difference between your fingers.

# STACKED KINGS

## You Will Need:

- one deck of cards

Remove a mystery card from the deck. The spectator chooses a card and uses that card to find two more. All three cards are Kings and the missing King turns out to be the mystery card.

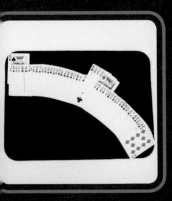

**1** Beforehand put the King of Spades (KS) on the top of the deck. Then in the following order stack the King of Clubs (KC), King of Hearts (KH), a random card and the King of Diamonds (KD) in the centre of the deck.

**2** Spread through the cards with faces towards you and **upjog** the KD. As you do this, break the deck in half between the KC and KH. Keep the KC on the face of the lower half. Break the deck here and pull out the KD with your left hand. Place it onto the table face down. This is the mystery card.

**3** As you put the deck back together, turn the pile in your left hand face down and put the right hand pile on top of those and keep a little **finger break**.

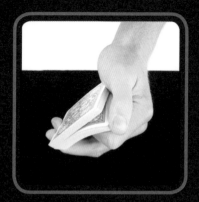

**TIP**

Try to time it so the spectator says 'stop' as you get to the centre of the deck near your break.

**4** The KD is now on the table. The KH is on top of the deck, the KC is on the bottom and the KS is in the middle below your little finger break.

**5** To force the KS, **riffle** your left thumb down the side of the deck and ask the spectator to call stop. No matter where they call stop, **cut** the cards at your break and hand the face down KS to the spectator. Tell them not to look at it yet.

**6** Ask the spectator to push their chosen card into the deck halfway.

**7** Spread the cards until you reach the chosen card. Cut the deck here and keep your left thumb on top of the chosen card as you turn the right hand packet face up and grip the chosen card with the right thumb.

**8** Turn the right hand over turning the chosen card end for end and showing the chosen card for the first time. Place the left hand packet on top of those. The other two kings are now secretly placed next to the KS in the spread.

**9** Turn the cards over and spread the deck face up to show that the spectator has pushed the king into the cards right next to two other Kings.

**10** Show the audience that they have found three of the Kings. Reveal that your mystery card was the 4th and final King all along.

# NUTS!

## You Will Need:

- four matching nuts from a hardware store

**Make nuts magically appear and disappear in your hand in front of an astonished audience.**

**1** Start with one nut loosely **finger palmed** in your left hand and three nuts on the table or in a spectator's hand.

**2** Pick up one nut and toss it into your open right hand. Count one, keeping your hand open.

**3** Pick up another nut. This time as you toss into your open right hand, secretly drop the finger palmed nut in as well. Count two, and immediate close your fist. This secret loads the third nut into your right hand.

**4** Take the third nut and put this in your pocket, but actually finger palm this nut.

**5** Ask the spectator how many nuts you have in your hand and they should say two. Tell them they were close and show all three nuts in your hand. Give them back to the spectator.

**6** Repeat the whole process, but this time actually put the third nut into your pocket. So now there are only three in play. The spectator may guess correctly this time as they are wise to your game, but that is okay.

**7** Now pick up one nut and **french drop** it, keeping the nut hidden in your left hand. Keep your right fingers closed now until the end of the trick.

**8** Pick up the last two nuts with your left hand, making sure you don't reveal the third nut. Put all three nuts into your pocket.

**9** Finally ask your spectator how many nuts you have. They may say one, two or three! It doesn't matter as you can now very cleanly show that all the nuts have vanished and your hands are empty!

# MULTIPLE OUTS

## You Will Need:

- four blank cards
- a marker pen
- one small envelope
- paper
- one fake banknote

Correctly predict which symbol the audience will choose out of four options. This trick uses the rule of multiple outs, so no matter what the audience chooses, your prediction will always be right.

*1* Take four blank cards and draw a random symbol on each. These are to be kept in a little envelope.

**TIP**
The symbols could be signs of the zodiac or logos.

*2* To prepare the 'outs', write on the back of the ball drawing, 'you will choose the ball'. On the flap of the envelope write 'you will choose the sun'. On a small piece of paper write 'you will choose the star'. Fold this up and put it inside the envelope. And finally on your fake money, write 'you will choose the flower'. Fold the note in half so the prediction is hidden.

*3* To perform the trick, bring out the envelope and remove the four symbol cards. Don't show the backs, the envelope flap or the hidden piece of paper. Tell the spectator they are going to make a choice and you bet you can predict their actions.

6 Then tell them to change their mind and choose another symbol and put their hand on it.

4 Bring out your fake money and tell them that this is what they can win.

5 Lay out the four cards carefully and ask the spectator to select one in their mind.

Practise this so you don't pull out the wrong prediction!

7 Give them one last chance to change their mind again. This should really convince them that they have a free choice – as they didn't even know what they'd choose, how could you! Once they are happy, reveal only the prediction that is correct (keep the other three incorrect predictions hidden!).

You will choose the sun

# ENVELOPE PEEK

## You Will Need:

- stack of blank cards
- three small envelopes
- three larger envelopes
- a marker pen
- craft knife

Any word or name is written onto a card, which is placed inside an envelope. Correctly reveal the secret information after playing a quick guessing game.

1 Cut a slit through the back of a small envelope as shown in the photo. This is your **gimmick** envelope with a super secret peeking device.

2 Collect two more small envelopes and three larger envelopes. Mark one of the larger envelopes with a dot in the top corner.

3 Ask a spectator to secretly write a word or name onto a blank card. While they are writing, show the small envelopes around, calling attention to the fact that they cannot be seen through.

**4** Insert the spectator's card, without looking at the writing, into the gimmick envelope through the slit. Make sure the card remains lined up with the edges of the envelope.

**5** Hold all three small envelopes in a fan facing the audience. You will now be able to see the word (through the envelope slit).

**6** Tell the audience you are going to play a game with the spectator. Place each small envelope into a large envelope. Make sure that you put the gimmick envelope into the envelope marked with a dot.

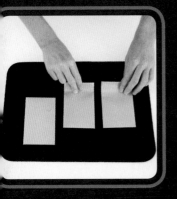

**7** Seal these envelopes and mix them up behind your back so the spectator doesn't know where their information is.

**8** Ask the spectator to choose two envelopes. If they choose the two envelopes not marked, tell them to hand them to people in the audience to open, leaving them with the marked envelope. Or the spectator will pick up one of each, marked and not marked. Ask them to hand you one of those. Whichever way they do it, your goal is to force the marked envelope on the spectator.

**9** Now for the big finish! You can reveal the information because you peeked earlier on! Place your hand on the marked envelope to get a 'psychic' read. Or write the information on a notepad to show the audience. Take the envelope from the spectator and carefully remove the smaller envelope with the information inside. Make sure you don't flash your gimmick. Show that the information matches!

# PENCIL THROUGH BANKNOTE

## You Will Need:

- a pencil
- one banknote
- a craft knife
- sticky note or paper

A pencil is pushed through the centre of a banknote, yet the note is unharmed.

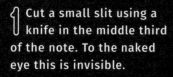

1 Cut a small slit using a knife in the middle third of the note. To the naked eye this is invisible.

2 Take out the **gimmick** note, a pencil and a small piece of paper. Fold the paper around the note and then fold both of them in half so the slit side is facing you.

3 Next pretend to insert the pencil in between the note and paper. You really thread the pencil through the slit, so when it reaches the fold it only makes contact with the paper.

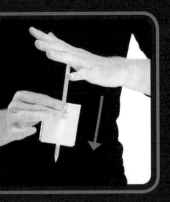

4 Stab the pencil through the note. This will create a convincing illusion from all **angles** that the pencil has pierced both the banknote and paper.

5 Remove the pencil and hand the paper to the spectator to show the hole.

6 Magically rub the bank note to restore it.

7 As you show the banknote to your audience, cover the slit with your fingers (but nobody is really looking for a tiny slit, as they are expecting a whopping great hole!).

# COIN VANISH

## You Will Need:

- one small coin
- a deck of cards or a similar size prop (e.g. a mobile phone)

**Make an ordinary coin vanish and reappear, then magically turn it into a deck of cards.**

**1** To start with, your deck of cards must be in your back trouser pocket. This is vital for the final part of this trick.

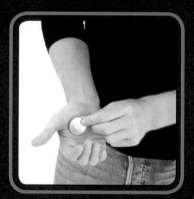

**2** Hold a coin at your left fingertips. Place the coin onto your right palm and as the bottom edge of the coin hits your palm, turn the coin towards the base of your hand and at the same time close your right fingers.

**3** Just as the coin goes out of sight, extend your left second, third and little fingers around the coin and steal it back into the left hand. Hold the coin at fingertip rest.

**4** Next push the coin into **classic palm** as the left hand lifts up and the left fingers extend to make a magical pass over the right hand.

**5** Show the right hand is empty and the coin has vanished and drop the left hand with the palmed coin to your side.

**6** Lift up both hands with palms facing you, fingers open and the coin resting on your left palm to show the coin has really gone.

**7** As you relax your hands back to your sides, let the coin drop from classic palm to **finger palm**.

**TIP**

This is called the retention vanish. To get a feel for it, practise actually placing the coin from one hand to the other without stealing it away. This will help your timing and tempo.

**8** Reach under your right thigh to find the coin. As you do this, your right hand reaches into your back pocket and gets your deck of cards.

**9** Keep the deck hidden in your right hand. Focus your attention on the coin as you pretend to toss it into your right hand. Really you keep the coin finger palmed in the left hand as you rotate your right palm upwards to reveal the deck.

# COIN IN A DRINKS CAN

## You Will Need:

- one sealed drinks can
- one small coin
- a marker pen
- a large glass

A coin is pushed through the bottom of a sealed drinks can!

1 Borrow a coin from a member of the audience and ask them to sign it.

### TIP

Be careful of your angles. Done well, it will look like the coin has gone as you can immediately show your hand is empty.

2 Hold the can with the base upright in one hand and the signed coin in the fingers of your other hand and pretend to throw the coin into the can. Really you slam the coin into the recess at the bottom of the can and keep it balanced there.

3 Transfer the can into your other hand. Draw attention to the top of the can and that it is sealed. As you do this, the coin will fall out of the bottom of the can and into your **finger palm.**

4 Now flip the can around to show the bottom is normal too, keeping the coin hidden. Sneaky, eh!

5 Give the can a little shake and allow the coin to tap against the metal so it sounds like the coin is really inside the can.

6 Then as you pull the ring on the can to open it, drop the coin into the can from finger palm. The fizz of the liquid will be enough misdirection for you to do this.

7 Pour out all of the liquid into the glass. Give the can one more shake so the audience can hear the coin inside.

8 Hand the can to the original spectator and ask them to remove the coin and confirm that it's their signed coin!

# WATCH HANDS PREDICTION

## You Will Need:

- two borrowed watches (one with a date winder)

## The spectator chooses a random time – and your watch matches it!

1 Set one of the watches to a random time and remember that time. Place it face down or out of sight.

2 Hold a second watch with the crown winder open. Twist the crown to move the hands around. You have the crown pulled out fully so the audience can see the hands moving around.

3 Distract the audience's attention away from the watch, and quickly set the time to match the other watch. Push the crown in one notch so now the hands won't move, only the date will.

**TIP**

Set the second time about a minute ahead of the first so the other watch catches up.

**4** Pass the watch to a spectator and ask them to put the watch behind their back and twist the crown around as many times as they like. Then when they are happy, push it back in. The spectator can move the crown around as much as they like without affecting the time.

**5** When the two watches are brought together you can show that the times match!

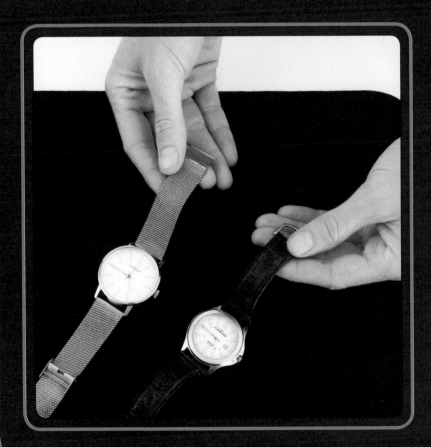

**TIP**

It is best to borrow a watch from one person and do the trick with someone else, as they may not know how the watch works.

You've put in the hard work behind the scenes, so remember to enjoy the audience's reactions at the end of your show. You deserve it! Chat to the audience afterwards and ask about their favourite pieces of magic. You'll be surprised at how much you can learn from their comments.

This is it, the big finish. The piece of magic that your audience will remember most vividly. Every finale here is spectacularly baffling. Give it everything you've got and bring it home.

# FINALES

# PHOTO PREDICTION

## You Will Need:

- a borrowed camera phone
- one deck of cards

**Predict a randomly chosen card from a photo taken before the trick even started!**

1 Before the trick starts, pull out any card you like from the deck and ask the spectator to hold it facing away from them for a photo. This will be your **force card**.

 2 Now place it back in the pack and ask for the cards to be **shuffled**.

 3 Take back the deck and fan the cards towards you to look for your force card.

**4** **Cut** the force card to the top of the deck.

**5** Ask the spectator to cut the cards into two piles. Place the bottom pile on top of the upper pile at an angle to 'mark' where the spectator cut, using the **cross cut force**.

**6** To force the card, draw your attention back to the deck and lift up the now top half and ask the spectator to take a look at the card they cut too. This is actually the force card, which started on top of the deck.

**TIP**

Use time misdirection between the force and the reveal so the audience forgets what happened.

**7** Invite them to show the card around and then to look at your photo prediction. When they zoom in, they will see the predicted card and the card they chose perfectly match.

# CARDS ACROSS

## You Will Need:

- one deck of cards that fits the size of your hand

**Cards are magically teleported from one spectator's hands to another's.**

1 Ask a spectator to stand on your left and **shuffle** the cards. They should then deal ten cards into your left hand. As they deal the eighth card, pretend to keep the cards square, but actually **injog** the card slightly, as they deal the ninth and tenth cards.

2 Now pull up on the top three cards with your right hand and catch a little **finger break**. Then extend your left third finger and push the cards up in the palm, to top palm the cards. Hold the remaining cards between your thumb and first finger to keep your right hand looking natural.

3 Give the pile of cards (which is now seven cards) to a spectator on your right.

4 Relax your right hand, which is palming three cards, to your side as you hold out your left hand and ask the spectator to deal another ten cards into your left hand.

**5** Once they have done this, bring your hands together naturally and add the three palmed cards to the top of the pile of ten (making 13 cards).

**6** Now swap cards with the spectator on your left.

**7** Go over what has happened with your audience. Spread through the remainder of the deck and locate any three, such as the Three of Clubs (3C). **Cut** it to the bottom, without the audience seeing the card.

**TIP**

Banter with the audience!

**8** Hold the cards longways in **biddle grip** with your right hand. Ask another spectator to come up and stand on your right. Begin to strip cards from the top with your left hand and ask the new spectator to call 'stop'.

**9** When they do, stop pulling cards and turn the right hand outwards to show the 3C. Say that the suit isn't important, just the number. Look at the number and act surprised.

**10** Tell the audience that you will magically make three cards teleport from the spectator on your left into the hands of the spectator on your right. Making the three cards teleport from one person to another is really magic. You need to really ham up your ability to make the cards invisibly fly across. Try mime and funny gestures!

# ORIGAMI PREDICTION

## You Will Need:

- two pieces of paper cut into matching squares (20x20cm)
- a glue stick
- twenty blank cards
- a marker pen
- a pencil

Ask the audience to choose a random object, then take a blank piece of paper and fold it up slowly. When you unfold the paper, it has transformed to show a picture of the audience's random object!

1 Beforehand, write a list of ten random objects (objects, places or people) onto cards. Then write a **forced** item onto another ten cards. Add a small pencil dot to the top corner of these forced cards. Stack the cards so the real items are on the bottom and the force cards are on the top.

2 Also beforehand, prepare two pieces of square paper that are identical in size: one is blank and one contains a picture of the force item. Fold them up and stick their top corners together as in the photo.

3 Now for the trick! Show some of the different cards to the audience.

**4** Ask a spectator to shuffle the cards. If a marked forced card is not on the top, ask them to cut the cards or **shuffle** them again, until a forced card is on top.

**5** Tell them to take the top card, show it around, and remember it.

**6** Now show the blank side of the square paper. Keep the folded force side hidden at the back in your hand. Fold the paper up into eighths and flip it over. This swaps the sides around.

**7** With a magical wave, unfold the paper to reveal the magical prediction!

# ZIPLOCK FORCE BAG

## You Will Need:

- two ziplock freezer bags (20x20cm)
- a glue stick
- double-sided tape
- plain paper
- a pen

Ask the audience to choose a random song, and predict the song correctly by sending a YouTube link of the track to the audience!

1 To make the prop, stick two ziplock freezer bags together so they are back-to-back. So you will have a bag with two pockets, although your audience will think there is one!

2 Cut some paper up into small pieces. Write some popular song names on the pieces. Fold them all up and put them into one side of the ziplock bag.

3 Now cut up some more paper into pieces. Write your **force** song on every single one! Put these into the other side of the force bag.

### TIP
Stick the ziplock bags together with a glue stick and a tiny amount of sticky tape around three edges.

4 In your performance send a link to the force song via YouTube or Spotify to someone in the audience. Tell them not to look at it yet.

5 Ask a few people in the audience to reach into the ziplock bag and pull out a piece of paper each. Make sure they only take a piece from the random side. Get them to call out their songs to show that they are all different. Get them to return the pieces to the same side.

6 Now ask someone else to take a piece of paper. But secretly turn the ziplock bag around so this person chooses from the force side. Have them call out their song.

NICE FOR WHAT

7 Finally ask the person to whom you sent the link to reveal the prediction.

TIP

This trick works well on stage as a finale. Play the song loudly to end your show as you take applause!

# WILL THE PHOTO MATCH?

## You Will Need:

- four printed photos

Four photos are torn in half and mixed up. Incredibly, at the end of the trick the pieces match. To start, hand the photos to a spectator to mix face down. Then ask them to follow the steps below...

1 Tear the photos in half widthways and stack one half on top of the other.

2 Cut the small pile of torn photos and complete the cut.

3 Spread the photos. Take the top three pieces and bury them anywhere into the middle of the spread.

4 Remove the top piece, which will be the chosen piece. Place it to one side, face down.

5 Bury the top piece into the middle of the fanned photos.

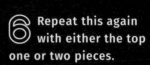

6 Repeat this again with either the top one or two pieces.

7 Throw the top one, two or three pieces onto the floor.

8 Move one piece from the top to the bottom, for each day of the week (seven times).

9 Now play 'she loves me, she loves me not'. For 'she loves me', place one piece from the top to the bottom. For 'she loves me **not**', take the top piece and throw it away.

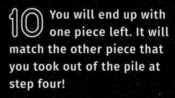

10 You will end up with one piece left. It will match the other piece that you took out of the pile at step four!

# COIN TO IMPOSSIBLE LOCATION

## You Will Need:

- one borrowed coin
- two identical napkins
- another coin
- a glue stick
- three boxes that fit inside one another
- a marker pen

A coin is borrowed and signed. It vanishes completely from the spectator's hands and reappears inside a sealed box.

**1** Beforehand, stick a coin on one of the napkins, slightly off centre. Then stick the other napkin over the top to hide the coin. Make sure the boxes are out of view of your audience, under a table or inside your magic case.

**2** To begin the trick, ask for a coin that roughly matches the size of the coin in the **gimmick** napkin. Ask a spectator to sign the coin.

**3** Show both sides of th napkin to your audience. Then place the signed coin into the napki and fold it over.

**4** Pass the napkin to a spectator. As you do this, secretly remove the signed coin in **finger palm** so they will be holding onto the concealed coin.

**5** Walk over to your boxes and slide the coin inside the smallest then nest the lids closed. When doing this trick, the blue boxes are actually inside the white box.

**6** To make the coin vanish, pinch hold of one of the corners of the napkin. Ask the spectator to let go of the coin. They will expect the coin to fall onto the floor but it will stay inside the napkin and look like it just vanished.

**7** Put the napkin away in your pocket. Draw attention to the box and reveal the coin inside.

## TIP
You can load the signed coin anywhere you like. Your audience doesn't know the coin has gone anywhere yet!

## TIP
This trick works great as a finale. You can make the coin vanish early on and then later in your show come back to the box to show the coin has reappeared.

# BIG SURPRISE

## You Will Need:

- one ten pence
- double sided tape
- three pennies
- one Rubik's cube
  (or other small item)

Using a few coins, play a guessing game with the audience. At the end of the trick a Rubik's cube or other prop will appear in a spectator's hand!

**1** Make a secret **gimmick** beforehand. Stick a penny to the back of a 10p.

**2** Begin with all the coins and the Rubik's cube in your right pocket. Reach into your pocket and have the penny and 10p at your fingertips, while keeping the other penny concealed in your hand as you place the coins into your left palm. Make sure the stuck penny is downwards out of sight.

**3** Ask the audience how much the coins add up to. They should say 11p. Take away the penny and secretly load the other penny into your closed hand. To do this, pick up the penny between your first finger and thumb as you extend the other three fingers to let the hidden penny fall in its place.

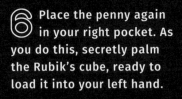

6 Place the penny again in your right pocket. As you do this, secretly palm the Rubik's cube, ready to load it into your left hand.

4 Turn your left hand downwards and close your fingers, showing the other coin in your right hand. Put this coin in your right pocket and ask again how much is left in your hand. The answer should be 10p.

5 Show that there is still 11p! Ask the spectator to take the penny from your left palm and hand it to you.

9 Turn your left hand downwards as you close your fingers. Place the gimmick coin cleanly in your right pocket.

7 Once again ask how much is there. Show you have 11p in your hand. Make sure as you open your fingers you flip the coin over so the stuck penny is now on display.

8 As you go to pick up this coin with your right first finger and thumb, extend your other fingers to let the Rubik's cube drop into your left hand secretly.

10 Finally, ask the spectator what is in your hand. There is no way they will be expecting a colourful Rubik's cube!

# ENVELOPE AND COINS PREDICTION

## You Will Need:

- large selection of coins
- five small envelopes
- five bulldog clips
- five drawing pins
- a cork noticeboard
- scissors
- paper for prediction
- a marker pen
- adhesive putty

Five small envelopes are opened, one at a time, to reveal a value of coins inside. Correctly predict the total inside the last envelope.

**1** Beforehand, stick five pins in the noticeboard, equal distance apart. This will be your back board for the trick.

**2** Write your prediction of **91p** on a large sheet of paper. Stick it to the back of your noticeboard with some adhesive putty.

**3** Put the following coins in five small envelopes (keep the coins in brackets to one side):

| | |
|---|---|
| Envelope 1 - 20p, 10p, 10p, 1p | (50p) |
| Envelope 2 - 50p, 5p, 5p, 10p | (20p + 1p) |
| Envelope 3 - 50p, 20p, 10p, 5p, 1p, 1p | (2p + 2p) |
| Envelope 4 - 20p, 20p, 20p, 10p, 5p, 2p, 2p | (10p + 2p) |
| Envelope 5 - 10p, 10p, 10p, 5p, 2p, 1p, 1p | (50p + 2p) |

**4** Before you close up each envelope, place the extra coin(s) inside, near the top and clip the envelope shut with a bulldog clip. There are some coins inside jingling around but one or two coins are trapped at the top by the bulldog clip.

**5** Hook all five envelopes onto your back board. You are now ready for the trick!

**6** Ask spectators to choose envelopes at random. Each time they pick an envelope, use the scissors to cut the envelope free from the clip below the extra coins. Keep the extra coins hidden! Have the audience count the coins inside to show they are random.

If you add up all the coins for each envelope, including the coins in brackets, each envelope adds up to 91p! This is part of the secret to the trick.

**7** Each time hand the cut envelope to a spectator to tip out the coins and count them. For the first four envelopes the totals will be different.

**8** For the last envelope however, unclip it from the bulldog clip and allow the extra coins to fall inside. This will make the total add up to your predicted 91p!

# ESPRESSO CUP AND BALL

## You Will Need:

- one takeaway espresso coffee cup
- one small ball (or something small, such as a sugar cube)
- one golf ball (or similar sized item)
- one Rubik's cube (or other small object)
- jacket with two outside pockets

An espresso cup is turned upside down and a spectator is invited to play a guessing game with a small ball. By the end of the trick, a golf ball and a Rubik's cube appear from under the cup.

**1** Beforehand, place the golf ball in your left outside jacket pocket and the Rubik's cube in your right outside pocket. The small ball is in the cup on the table.

**2** Invite your spectators to play a guessing game with you. Place your hand over the top of the cup and give it a shake so the audience can hear the small ball rattling inside.

**3** Turn the cup upside down. Pretend to take the small ball from the cup and put it in your left jacket pocket – leave your hand in there. Secretly leave the small ball inside the cup.

**4** Ask your audience if they think you took the small ball or if it's still under the cup. It doesn't matter what they answer, as this question directs their attention away from the magic that is about to happen.

**5** Slowly lift the cup up with your right hand just enough to let the small ball show underneath. At the same time, secretly grab the golf ball from your pocket and hold it in a loose palm with your left hand still inside your pocket.

**6** Lift up the cup to show the small ball and move it towards you. At the same time, bring the golf ball hidden in your hand from the pocket. Secretly sneak the golf ball inside the cup.

**7** Rest the cup on your left hand with the golf ball inside. Pick up the small ball with your right hand. Then put the cup back on the table with the left hand. Don't show that the golf ball is under there!

**8** Use your right hand to put the small ball into your right jacket pocket. Ask what's under the cup. Lift up the cup to reveal the golf ball!

**9** Loosely palm the Rubik's cube in your right hand. Move the cup towards you with your left hand and pop the cube into the cup.

**10** Put the cup containing the Rubik's cube back on the table. For the last time, can your audience guess what's under the cup? Slowly lift the cup to reveal the Rubik's cube.

# CONCLUSION

I hope you've enjoyed reading this book and you're well on your way to becoming a real magician. But don't worry if you can't get things right on your first try – or even your second, third, fourth or fifth tries – keep practising and stay positive. Practise getting the basic moves right first in simple tricks, and then move on to the more complicated tricks. It takes a lot of practice to become a slick and polished magician! And you never stop learning, as there's always a new trick or a new way of doing magic to learn.

In addition to the tricks in this book, look on the internet. There are hundreds of tricks with videos that demonstrate magic online. My advice is to start with books and videos that contain lots of tricks (a magician's whole **repertoire**). Usually the magician has put more effort into using the material in the real world for real people. Seek out magic lectures that you can download. These contain hours of content and you will be learning first hand from some excellent magicians.

My aim with this book was to inspire you to become the best magician you can be. To do that, you must always be curious about magic and about life. Inspiration for tricks can be found everywhere. Make a note of anything that interests you, take photos and keep cuttings from magazines and newspapers. And look at my suggestions in this book for turning your interests into tricks.

Finally, I'd like to pass on some advice that a very good magician once gave to me about performing tricks:

**you have to say what you mean, mean what you say and you have to try**. I'll explain what this means to me... try to be clear with your audience and make the tricks simple to understand, even if the method is sometimes difficult. Deliver your tricks with confidence and trust that you will astound your audience. Lastly, the audience can sense when someone has put in the hard work to learn their craft. If they can feel the effort you are putting in, they will love you for it and respond wonderfully. Enjoy the magic, make magic and share magic.

**JB**

# MAGICIAN'S CHECKLIST

**Use this step-by-step guide as a final checklist of things you need to do before your show...**

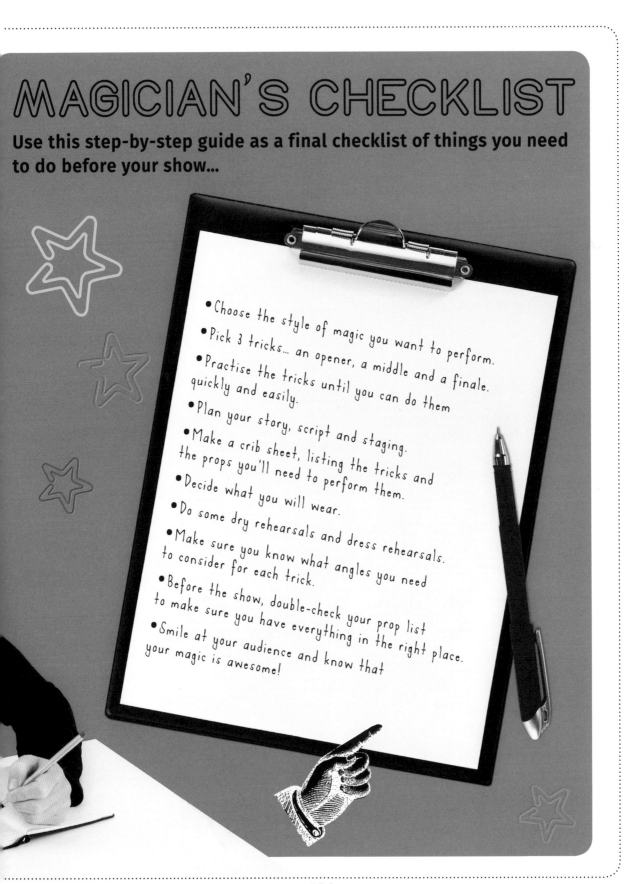

- Choose the style of magic you want to perform.
- Pick 3 tricks... an opener, a middle and a finale.
- Practise the tricks until you can do them quickly and easily.
- Plan your story, script and staging.
- Make a crib sheet, listing the tricks and the props you'll need to perform them.
- Decide what you will wear.
- Do some dry rehearsals and dress rehearsals.
- Make sure you know what angles you need to consider for each trick.
- Before the show, double-check your prop list to make sure you have everything in the right place.
- Smile at your audience and know that your magic is awesome!

# GLOSSARY

**ANGLES**
The sight lines of the audience.

**BIDDLE GRIP**
An overhand grip that keeps control of the top cards.

**BOBO SWITCH**
A method of secretly switching one object for another.

**CLASSIC PALM**
To hide something in the palm of your hand.

**CRIB SHEET**
A cue card that contains information about the order of your magic show. Very useful for performances.

**CROSS CUT FORCE**
A method of forcing a playing card on top of the deck.

**CUT**
To split a deck of cards into two.

**DEALER'S GRIP**
A way to hold cards in your hands naturally, like a dealer in a casino would.

**DRESS REHEARSAL**
A full rehearsal of your show, wearing the outfit you'll be performing in and using all of the actual props.

**DRY REHEARSAL**
A quicker rehearsal where you run through just the parts of your show that you think need work.

**FALSE CUT**
A way of cutting the cards that does not actually alter the order of the whole deck.

**FALSE TRANSFER**
When the magician pretends to put an item in their hand but actually retains it in the other.

**FINGER BREAK**
Using a finger to keep a gap between two parts of a deck of cards.

**FINGER PALM**
To hide an object in folded-over fingers.

**FLIP STICK**
A move that can make a pen or other similar shaped object disappear at your fingertips.

**FORCE**
An object that a volunteer thinks they pick, but is actually controlled by the magician.

**FRENCH DROP**
A way to make a coin vanish.

**GIMMICK**
Specially-made object that looks normal, but has special features for doing magic tricks.

**HAN PING CHIEN**
The loading of a coin or other small object into the magician's closed fist, named after a famous coin wizard.

**INJOG**
Pulling one card inwards, closer to your body to mark its position.

**MATERIALISE**
To appear as if from empty air.

**MISDIRECTION**
To control the audience's attention.

**MUSCLE MEMORY**
The ability to perform sleight of hand without giving too much thought to what your hands are actually doing.

## OVERHAND INJOG SHUFFLE

A way of shuffling the cards to control a particular card or stack of cards.

## RAMSAY SUBTLETY

A method of showing your hands are 'empty', even though you are finger palming a coin.

## REPERTOIRE

The entirety of a magician's tricks.

## RETENTION VANISH

A method of vanishing a coin.

## RIFFLE SHUFFLE

A method for shuffling the cards fairly.

## SHUFFLE

To rearrange the order of the cards completely at random.

## SHUTTLE PASS

A way of visually changing one object for another.

## SLEIGHT OF HAND

Fancy finger work such as palming a coin, controlling a chosen card or using your memory.

## SLIP CUT

A type of cut that only alters the position of the top card and buries it into the centre of the pack.

## SWING CUT

A cut from one hand to the other, using your first finger to break the deck and swing it into your other hand.

## THUMB BREAK

A method of marking the place of a particular card in the deck by keeping a gap between packets.

## THUMB OFF

To push off the top card from the deck with your thumb from dealer's grip.

## VERNON TOUCH

A way of being so natural with your actions that your sleight of hand matches the actions you perform in everyday life.

# INDEX